D1308980

Under
the
Water

illustrated by Betsy Rotunno & Guy Wolek
written by Jenny & Dandi Mackall

Under the water waits a secret world of wonder and mystery. Dive on in, but beware! Amazing things go on down there.

Seahorses are the only fish that swim standing up. They can move their eyes separately to see in all directions at the same time.

You can see why
this bright little guy is
called a *clownfish*. He
spends his day eating
left-over fish.

The colorful *parrotfish* makes a lot of noise as it bites off chunks of coral. At night, some parrotfish make a clear bubble to sleep in.

Can you guess what the *sea cucumber* looks like? They swallow mud from the ocean floor, keep the tiny animals that live in the mud, then spit out the rest!

Most *starfish* have five "arms" that feel around for food. If one arm breaks, the starfish grows another one.

It would be hard to be uglier than the *hagfish*.

ACHOOO

The hagfish clogs its own nostril with the slime it makes, then has to sneeze to clear its nose.

Jellyfish drift along in the water. With no bones, brain, or heart, the jellyfish looks like a blob. But it stings!

Up to a thousand *anchovies* swim together
in groups, called schools. Believe it or not,
some people like anchovies on their pizza!

The eight-legged *octopus* protects herself and her babies by changing shape, color, and feel, and by shooting out a dark ink. She is one of the world's best parents.

Some tropical *catfish* swim
upside down while they eat.
A marine catfish can taste with any part of its body.

Lanternfish create their own light as they swim. One fish makes enough light to let you read in bed at night.

The female *angler fish* has a "fishing line" with a lighted tip sticking out of her head.

Her big mouth lets her swallow curious fish twice her size!

The *fairy basslet* are colorful fish that can change from girls into boys! They range in size from less than an ounce to 700 pounds.

The world under the water is filled with different kinds of whales. Whales talk to each other in whistles, squeaks, clicks, and groans. Humpback whales sing!

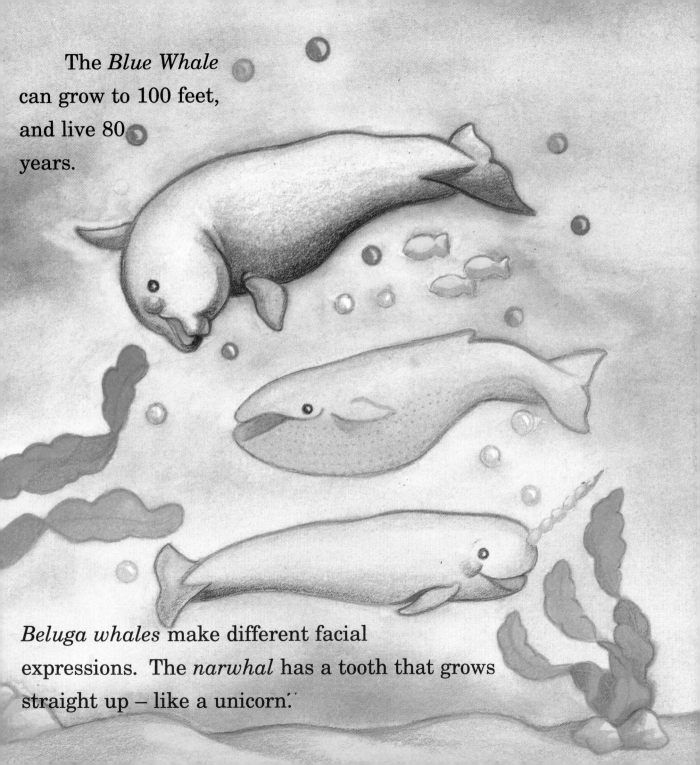

The *Blue Whale* can grow to 100 feet, and live 80 years.

Beluga whales make different facial expressions. The *narwhal* has a tooth that grows straight up – like a unicorn.

The *whale shark* is the largest fish. It weighs twice as much as an African elephant.

The *white shark* has teeth as hard as steel. They are always hungry, and they never get sick!

Dolphins, the smartest water animals, love to play tag
and dance on the water. *Bottlenose dolphins* have been
known to rescue humans and lead ships safely to harbor.

So grab your snorkel and your fins!
Dive in and start exploring.

An amazing animal world is
waiting for you just
under the water.

TRANSPORTATION

ILLUSTRATED BY ROBERT INGPEN
TEXT BY
PHILIP WILKINSON & MICHAEL POLLARD

CHELSEA HOUSE PUBLISHERS
New York • Philadelphia

First published in the United States in 1995 by
Chelsea House Publishers

First Printing
1 3 5 7 9 8 6 4 2

Simplified text and captions by **Michael Pollard**
based on the *Encyclopedia of Ideas that Changed the
World* by Robert Ingpen & Philip Wilkinson

Editor	Diana Briscoe
Project Editor	Claire Watts
Designer	Design 23
Art Director	John Strange
Design Assistants	Karen Fergusom
	Victoria Furbisher
DTP Manager	Keith Bambury
Editorial Director	Pippa Rubinstein

ISBN 0–7910–2768–6

Printed in Italy